Date _____

Dear

_____

_____

_____

_____

_____

From

_____

The Heart of a Teacher

Art and text © Karla Dornacher, licensed by Suzanne Cruise
Artwork and text licensed by J Countryman, used by permission.

© 2003 Christian Art Gifts, RSA
        Christian Art Gifts Inc., IL, USA

Designed by Christian Art Gifts

Printed in China

ISBN 1-86920-326-7

03 04 05 06 07 08 09 10 11 12 – 10 9 8 7 6 5 4 3 2 1

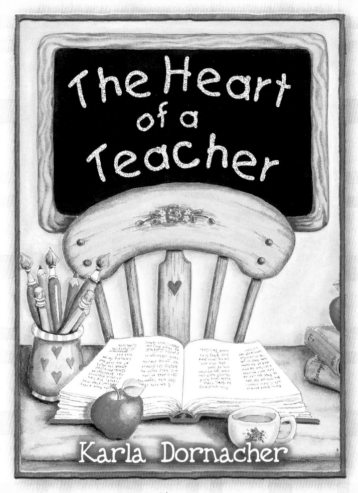

The Heart of a Teacher

Karla Dornacher

christian
art gifts

Your love has given me
great joy and encouragement.

Philemon 7

4

I wanted to swing so high in the sky,
the other kids could, I wanted to try.
I sat down alone and held on tight,
I kicked my feet with all my might.
But the swing stayed still, it didn't sway
and I learned a special lesson that day.

Sometimes we need a push to start,
a gentle nudge from a caring heart.
You saw in me the potential to soar
you encouraged me to try so much more!

Whenever I struggled, kicking my feet,
you never let me give up in defeat.
So thank you, Teacher, for giving me
the push I needed to be all I could be.

Thank you, Teacher...

for loving me unconditionally...

for encouraging me to grow in
the gifts God has given me...

for helping me run the race
of life without giving up...

for making me feel like a
winner when I do my
best and don't give in...

for teaching me truth with
wisdom and understanding...

for preparing me to walk with
confidence and courage into
a world of endless opportunities.

God created me to be one of a kind.
There's no one else like me!
I can do some things really good.
But some things,
no matter how hard I try,
I will never be good at.
That's just the way God made me.
I'm glad you don't expect me
to be someone I'm not,
but you always encourage me
to be the best me I can be.
Thank you!

Aa Bb Cc Dd Ee
Ff Gg Hh Ii Jj
wisdom
is better
than
wealth

I am fearfully
and wonderfully
made.

Psalm 139:14

9

Apple Muffin Mix

Sparkling
cider

To-
From-

Heavenly Chip Co.
Apple Chips

A-tisket, a-tasket,
A teacher's apple basket,
A token of our gratitude
To honor your great attitude!

*From the fruit of his lips a
man is filled with good things
as surely as the work
of his hands rewards him.*

Proverbs 12:14

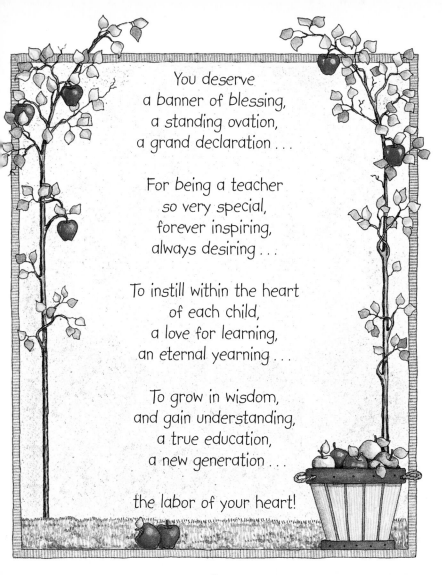

You deserve
a banner of blessing,
a standing ovation,
a grand declaration . . .

For being a teacher
so very special,
forever inspiring,
always desiring . . .

To instill within the heart
of each child,
a love for learning,
an eternal yearning . . .

To grow in wisdom,
and gain understanding,
a true education,
a new generation . . .

the labor of your heart!

Core Values

Do unto others as you would like them

Love

Honor

Respect

Patience

Honesty

Kindness

Gentleness

Compassion

to do unto you.

Luke 6:31

14

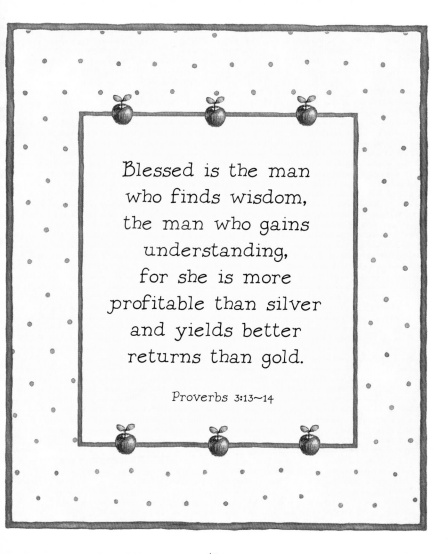

Blessed is the man
who finds wisdom,
the man who gains
understanding,
for she is more
profitable than silver
and yields better
returns than gold.

Proverbs 3:13~14

For He shall give
His angels
charge over you,
to keep you
in all your ways.

Psalm 91:11, NKJV

16

Great are the works
of the LORD;
they are pondered
by all
who delight in them.

Psalm 111:2

It is no accident
you're my teacher.
God knew you were
the perfect one.
He gave you the passion
to mold and shape me,
to challenge my mind
and make it fun.

I know at times
you must grow weary,
with all the work
you have to do;
so I pray for God
to give you rest
so you don't give up . . .
because I need you!

You're a special person

a teacher who truly cares

please know you're appreciated

and daily in our prayers

Dear Jesus,

Bless this teacher
with the light of Your love,
a heavenly vision – a gift from above.

Give her eyes to see, Lord, what no one else can
that spark of the future she holds in her hand.

May she catch a glimpse of lives yet untold,
bright hope for tomorrow in each child to unfold.

May she shine like a star, reflecting Your glory,
as she is a chapter in each child's lifelong story.

Amen

You shine like stars in the universe
as you hold out the word of life.

Philippians 2:15

21

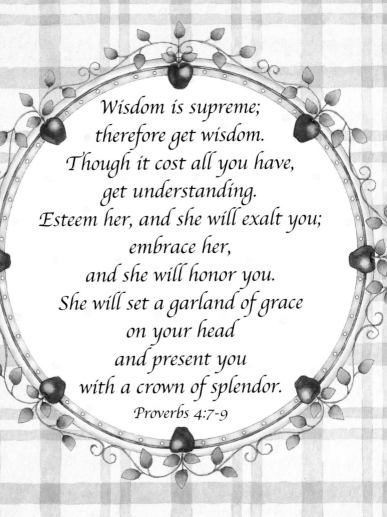

Wisdom is supreme;
therefore get wisdom.
Though it cost all you have,
get understanding.
Esteem her, and she will exalt you;
embrace her,
and she will honor you.
She will set a garland of grace
on your head
and present you
with a crown of splendor.

Proverbs 4:7-9

The fear of the Lord
is the beginning of knowledge
and the hope
of the next generation.

We thank God for giving
us teachers like you
who build on this
solid foundation.

Dear Jesus,

Thank You for this teacher
and all the love and energy
she pours into each child
You've placed in her care.

I ask You, Lord,
to replenish her strength this day.
Pour out, into her life,
a drink of refreshing and blessing
that will fill her cup
and overflow her heart!
Amen.

You color my life . . .

with faith to believe
in the unbelievable . . .

with hope for a world
lost and hopeless . . .

with love to reach
out to the unloveable . . .

and color my world
with a touch of God.

You color my
life with joy!

COLORS

 You make a difference!

Be of good courage,
and He shall
strengthen
your heart,
all you who hope
in the LORD.

Psalm 31:24, NKJV

29

A is for Apples and Angels...

they're both sweet and so are you!

B is for Birds and Blessings...

singing the praises of all you do!

You are an ABC of a Teacher

You Accept each one of us for who we are with our individual weaknesses, strengths, and unique God~given personalities.

You Bless us with your passion and enthusiasm to share the wonders of the universe in ways that stir our desire for more.

You Challenge our hearts to pursue the love of learning, our minds to explore the world around us, and our spirits to seek truth above all else.

God bless Teachers

Karla Dornacher

"May the LORD
bless you
and protect you.

May the LORD
smile on you
and be gracious
to you.

May the LORD
show you His favor
and give you
His peace."

Numbers 6:24~26, NLT

I applied my heart
to what I observed
and learned a lesson
from what I saw.
~ Proverbs 24:32

Thank you, Teacher, . . .
for you've been a great example
as I've watched you day by day.
You don't just teach me by the book,
it's more than what you say . . .
it's how your heart communicates
through your actions and your caring,
that helps me apply to my life
the knowledge that you're sharing.

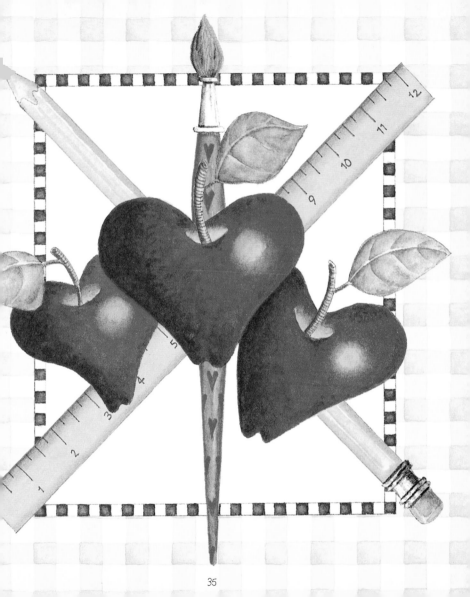

35

Wisdom

She is a tree of life
to those who embrace her;
those who lay hold of
her will be blessed...

The righteous eat
to their hearts' content.

Proverbs 3:18; 13:25

You are
God's
workmanship . . .

. . . created in Christ Jesus to do
good works, which God prepared
in advance for you to do!
(from Ephesians 2:10)

We thank God
for you and the good work
you do teaching minds,
touching hearts,
and taking the time to care!

Our children enter your classroom
with countless questions to be asked,
seeking honest answers and wise counsel,
knocking on the doors
of their futures yet unknown.

We are thankful that God
has entrusted you
with the knowledge to answer the questions,
the wisdom to guide and direct,
and the key to open the door
to the next step of their journey.

A good rule of thumb
is to measure one's heart
with the yardstick of giving.

"If you give, you will receive.
Your gift will return to you
in full measure,
pressed down, shaken together
to make room for more, and running over.
Whatever measure you use in giving ~
large or small ~
it will be used to measure
what is given back to you."

Luke 6:38, NLT

Thank you, Teacher,
for giving so much of yourself to me!

Reading, 'riting and 'rithmetic
are the basics of good education.
They are the skills our minds will use
to live a life of exploration.

For the future is filled with treasures
far greater than silver and gold ~
a wealth of knowledge to discover ~
the riches of wisdom untold.

So thank you, Teacher, for all you do,
for laying a solid foundation,
for paving the path to all my tomorrows
with hope in the next generation!

Now faith is the substance of things hoped for, the evidence of things not seen.

Hebrews 11:1, NKJV

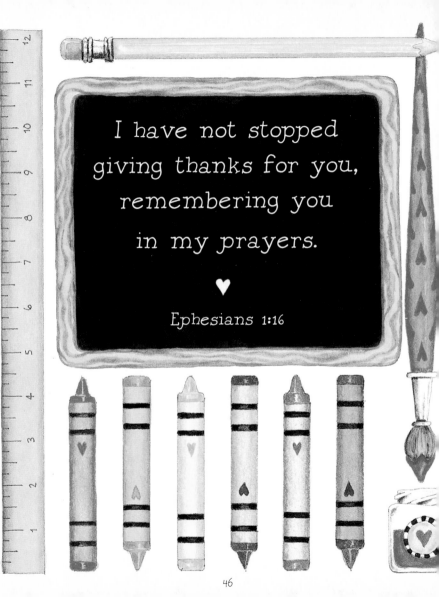

I have not stopped
giving thanks for you,
remembering you
in my prayers.

♥

Ephesians 1:16

Dear Teacher,
You don't know me... not really.
You don't know my inner thoughts
or secret fears.
You don't know how much I struggle
to be liked and accepted.
You don't know how much I want
someone to see me and believe in me.

But when you
smile at me and
say "you can do it,
I know you can",
I feel special...
and I think you
know more than
I think you know.

COLORS